THE RACE SET BEFORE US

A Devotional Guide for Runners

Also by Paula Wiseman

Fiction

    The Covenant of Trust Series

        Contingency

        Indemnity

        Precedent

        Sanction

    The Foundations Series

        Razed

        Refined

        Resolute

    The Encounters Series

        Touched

        Embraced

Devotional

        56 Tips to Help You Get the Most Out of Every Book in the Bible

THE RACE SET BEFORE US

A Devotional Guide for Runners

PAULA WISEMAN

SAGE

WORDS

ROBINSON, ILLINOIS

Paula Wiseman
Sage Words
606 N. Cross Street
Robinson, IL 62454
www.paulawiseman.com

Unless otherwise noted Scripture taken from the *New King James Version*. Copyright © 1979, 1980, 1982 by Thomas Nelson, Inc. Used by permission. All rights reserved. Scripture quotations marked ESV are from the *ESV® Bible (The Holy Bible, English Standard Version®)*, copyright © 2001 by Crossway, a publishing ministry of Good News Publishers. Used by permission. All rights reserved. Scripture quotations marked NLT are taken from the *Holy Bible*, New Living Translation, copyright © 1996, 2004. Used by permission of Tyndale House Publishers, Inc., Carol Stream, Illinois 60188. All rights reserved. Scripture quotations marked NAS are taken from the *New American Standard Bible®*, Copyright © 1960, 1962, 1963, 1968, 1971, 1972, 1973, 1975, 1977, 1994 by The Lockman Foundation. Used by permission. Other Scripture taken from *THE MESSAGE*, Copyright © 1993, 1994, 1995, 1996, 2000, 2001, 2002. Used by permission of NavPress Publishing Group.

Cover photo from Fotolia.com.

For more information, visit paulawiseman.com or email paula@paulawiseman

Book Layout © 2014 BookDesignTemplates.com

The Race Set Before Us/Paula Wiseman. -- 1st ed.
ISBN 978-0-9986505-0-0

For Jon

Do you not know that those who run in a race all run, but one receives the prize? Run in such a way that you may obtain it.

—1 CORINTHIANS 9:24

CONTENTS

Foreword

One of my running heroes is the Scottish missionary, Eric Liddell. In the 1924 Olympics, he missed his strongest event, the 100-meter, because of his conviction about the holiness of the Sabbath. Immediately before the 400-meter race, he received a note referencing 1 Samuel 2:30, *"those who honor me I will honor."* Inspired, Eric won the gold medal and set a new world record posting a personal best by a miraculous two seconds. In the movie *Chariots of Fire* he says, "I believe God made me for a purpose, but He also made me fast. And when I run I feel His pleasure." This statement exudes a beautiful authenticity considering that Eric not only missed an Olympic race for his faith but also died as a missionary martyr in a Chinese World War II concentration camp.

Running, like other sports, provides a concentrated life experience. A football game or a marathon can be framed as a distillation of our life story, condensed into a few hours. Races and games reinforce our concepts of insurmountable obstacles, shining moments, and exuberant winners. Coaches and spectators recall the good, bad, and ugly in expanded detail. The runner evaluates his training, effort, and fortune in the context of a race. Similarly, Christian growth has outward indications of progress, but the more poignant modifications are known only to the individual Christian.

Our Heavenly Father employs our human efforts in virtually all His plans. To become a more effective instrument of God, we must confront our sluggish nature so we can unleash the dynamo wonderfully installed by our Creator. Running is the simplest, most fundamental expression of human physical effort. And while I don't think that God favors runners, I do think that God rewards the human ideal of maximum effort when it is tempered with God's ideal of altruism.

About a year before I was encouraged to start running by a coworker, I watched my uncle die of pancreatic cancer. His prayer two days prior to his heavenly departure affirmed his lifelong faith that *"all things work together for good for those that love God."* Seeing his bold faith gave me reason to question my reliance on God. Could I see the goodness if I was certain the end of my life was near? The realization that life gets harder and not easier as we progress through life provided a seed in my psyche that allowed me to say yes to the running invitation.

In running, I have found a pastime. So, when I found out that Paula was writing a new book intertwining running and Biblical truths in an ADD-friendly, short-chapter format, I was beyond excited. She shines a spotlight on the beautiful intersection of running and the truths of the Bible. This book might make you a better runner, but it is certain to increase your appreciation of how running can provide insight in your quest for spiritual growth.

Jay Hawkins

Introduction

Let me say up front, I am not a great runner. I'm not even a good runner. But I run anyway. When I started just after my forty-first birthday I envisioned that time becoming a tremendous opportunity to talk to God, to enjoy the early morning quiet, and have some me time.

In those early days, my prayers consisted of important things like "Next . . . breath . . . God . . ." and "Let me get my phone out before the heart attack hits."

Important, maybe. Deeply spiritual, not so much.

I stayed with it, though, running and listening. Over the course of several years and more than a few miles, God has taught me some amazing lessons, about myself, about life and about this race we are all in.

In the pages that follow, I share some of those lessons. They range from simple to profound, from "everybody knows that" to "I never thought of that." More than anything, He taught me that He wants to speak if we want to listen. He wants to encourage if we dare to try. He wants us to endure if we choose to run.

". . . let us run with endurance the race that is set before us, looking unto Jesus . . ." Hebrews 12:1-2

1

Throw Out Your Expectations

According to my earnest expectation and hope that in nothing I shall be ashamed, but with all boldness, as always, so now also Christ will be magnified in my body, whether by life or by death. Philippians 1:20

Remember I said I expected to have this super-spiritual time during my run? Didn't happen.

I also expected to lose weight. Didn't happen.

I also found out if you have never run, forty-five seconds is embarrassingly challenging.

I quickly learned running was new territory and previously held ideas and standards no longer applied. Sure, I could *walk* three or four miles, no trouble.

Running was different.

In the race God has set before us, whether we are new believers, or we have been at this for years, we bring an armload of expectations with us, expectations that, when unmet, damage our faith.

Drop those expectations.

We hold on to things like "now that I'm a believer, things will get easier." And when the opposite happens, we are swallowed up with "why did You let this happen to me?"

We have ideas about how God should let us serve Him. When He wants to take us in a new and different direction, we resist or even refuse.

We have notions about what our results should be, and we measure our "success" or "failure" by our standards, rather than God's.

Living in a way that honors God is different from any other approach to life.

So what standards and preconceived ideas do we draw on? Personal experience. Historical examples. Business models that don't always work, teaching techniques that sometimes fail, and marketing strategies that often miss the mark.

Living a life of faith is different. It is constantly 'looking unto Jesus' and nowhere else, fixing and re-fixing our eyes on the author and finisher of our faith.

The more we cling to our expectations, the more we frustrate His purposes.

God's goal is making us more Christ-like, preparing each of us to serve Him through eternity. Our lives now are a wisp of a warm-up for our real calling. This is not the main event.

I forget that. Often.

Doing things God's way means that hard times bring joy and strength, while easy times make me lazy and prone to ignore God. Failing to meet a goal may actually mean success in the bigger picture because it means surrendering my plans to His.

In what ways has following Jesus been different than what you expected? Is it more difficult or less difficult? Is it harder to follow in the difficult times?

2

Gotta Be the Shoes

For shoes, put on the peace that comes from the Good News so that you will be fully prepared. Ephesians 6:15 NLT

Shoes matter. When I started running, it was pure, dumb luck that I had good shoes. However, when those sneakers wore out, so did my luck.

My second pair of shoes threw off my stride and caused some real pain on the insides of my calves. I quickly became educated about pronation, gait and support in my quest for the right shoe. It paid off. I have great shoes now, and pain in my feet ankles or knees is no longer an issue.

Scripture mentions shoes in a key passage in Ephesians 6. Paul discusses putting on the armor of God and mentions the *"preparation of the gospel of peace."* Granted, the combat shoes in Paul's analogy are a little different than running shoes, but the purpose is the same—**enabling you to move forward with traction and confidence**.

For that, your best choice, best fit is the gospel of Jesus Christ.

The Gospel of Jesus Christ—We know what it is. We understand we have been saved from eternal judgment, and that we have eternal life ahead of us, but do we realize what power if gives us NOW. The good news is

- that we are **forgiven** from every offense committed against a holy God,
- that we are **accepted**,
- that God **delights** in us just as He delights in His Son.

Not just on our good days. Every day. **Favored. Accepted. Loved**.

Walk in those shoes for a while. See if that doesn't help you move forward with traction and confidence.

Why do we forget who we are in Christ so quickly and easily? What confidence does your identity give you? Name one way the gospel empowers you today.

3

Running with a Plan

'For I know the plans that I have for you,' declares the *LORD, 'plans for welfare and not for calamity to give you a future and a hope.' Jeremiah 29:11 NAS*

When I started running, I knew less than nothing about what I was doing. My plan consisted of running as far as I could and then walking until I could breathe again.

Then one day, my husband brought me a real training plan. Following it, I learned I was able to push beyond what I thought I was capable of. I stretched out my distances, my recovery times improved, and so did my speed.

Granted, there were plenty of weeks I didn't reach all the goals the plan laid out for me. Sometimes, it took three or four weeks to accomplish what the plan slated for a single week. But having a concrete goal, and measurable progress helped me out tremendously.

When we become believers, we understand that means living a Christ-like life. And we get busy, doing the best we can. Success is spotty. Progress is hard to measure, and it's easy to get discouraged. This is where you need a plan. God gave us that plan in His Word.

You may be thinking there's no clear-cut plan in Scripture. (Not like Monday: Walk one mile. Run five minutes. Walk three minutes. Repeat three times. Walk one mile. Pretty straightforward.)

But as you read your Bible—just read, not deep study—as you listen to sermons, or go to a small group, things will catch your attention. It may be positive, like an exciting new insight. It may be negative, like an attitude that needs correction. Those things that you're drawn to, those are the things God wants you to work on next. This is your plan. God has tailor-made for you.

One area of my spiritual training God is working with me on is my worship. Sunday mornings are crazy, and by the time my brain has settled enough for worship, church is over. I want to come bringing acceptable praise, not just be "present." So my plan right now centers on these questions:

Where is my heart?

What are my priorities?

Why do I get off-track?

What changes do I need to make to my routine to be better prepared for worship?

When He's satisfied with my progress, He'll move me on to the next step in the plan. If He deems it necessary, we'll revisit this one, but ultimately it's part of His greater plan to make me more like Christ.

What's in your current training plan? Have you already worked through some training?

4

Breathing

And when He had said this, He breathed on them, and said to them, "Receive the Holy Spirit. John 20:22

The single most important factor that determines how far or how fast I run is not my heart rate or my leg muscles. It's not even the heat or the hills. It's not lack of hydration or my shoes that causes me to take a walking break.

It's breathing.

I knew breathing would be important, but I didn't realize what a make-or-break-you part of running it was. Once the newbie, gasping phase of running passed, I discovered there is a rhythm to it. That steady in and out increased my endurance far beyond what I believed I was capable of.

In the New Testament, the same Greek word, *pneuma*, is used for breath and Spirit, and there's a definite parallel between physical running and running the race God lays before us.

The key to success and endurance is learning to run in the rhythm the Holy Spirit dictates.

If I push too hard, my lungs can't keep up and I get that familiar pain in my side. In the same way, if I try to push beyond the Spirit's direction, He'll give me that hitch as a door closed, an obstacle in my way, the counsel of a godly friend, or sometimes a spectacular failure.

The "heat" and the "hills" are part of the course God chooses. I picked up my shoes already. But breathing well gives me the strength to keep moving.

In Matthew 11:29 The Message says, *"Walk with Me and work with Me—watch how I do it. Learn the unforced rhythms of grace."*

Breathing. In and out.

The Holy Spirit. In us, then out through us.

What interferes with the Holy Spirit's direction? What makes it difficult to hear His voice? What confirmation does He give that you're on the right track?

5

Results Vary

But you must continue to believe this truth and stand firmly in it. Don't drift away from the assurance you received when you heard the Good News. The Good News has been preached all over the world, and I, Paul, have been appointed as God's servant to proclaim it. Colossians 1:23 NLT

At one point during those early days, I was hoping to stretch out my morning run. Up to that point, nineteen minutes and a little over two miles had been my longest, but I wanted the two-mile mark to be comfortably attainable and not a personal best. So I boldly (real runners, don't laugh) set my timer for twenty-two minutes and headed out.

I ran a new route, so I'd focus more on my surroundings and less on huffing and puffing. Before I even realized it, I blew through the twenty-two minutes and then RESET my timer. I can remember checking my watch at one point, and thinking "Only eleven more minutes." Only! I finished the day after fifty-five minutes and nearly FIVE miles.

The next time I went out, it was all I could do to get a mile and a half in before taking a walking break. What happened?

For weeks after that, three miles was the best I could do. Decent maybe, but well short of five.

Results vary.

My Christian race is no different. I've had times of gradual progress, building and growing.

Occasionally I see mind-blowing leaps I didn't think were possible.

Sometimes, I have a disappointing season, with no success to show for my efforts.

Every once in a while, I even sleep in.

"But you're doing it."

That's what my husband—a much more experienced runner—tells me when I get aggravated by my lack of progress.

Getting out there. Making the effort. That's what counts. It's not the times, the distances, or the speed, it's the **running**.

Day in.
Day out.
Put on the shoes and go.

How difficult is it to keep going when you don't feel like you're having success in your Christian life? What reassurances and truths can you fall back on?

6

Stay in the Light

But if we walk in the light as He is in the light, we have fellowship with one another, and the blood of Jesus Christ His Son cleanses us from all sin. 1 John 1:7

At 5 a.m., it's dark. So from September to May, my running routes are limited to well-lit streets. (Well-lit, but without heavy traffic—a tricky combination.) This helps keep me safe and protects me from a fall or a turned ankle on uneven pavement.

Running (or walking) in the light is key to my Christian life as well. In 1 John 1:7, the apostle cites walking in the light as the mark of a genuine Christian.

What does it mean, then to "walk in the light"? Back in verse 5, John says God is light. So walking in the light means to walk "in God"—in His holiness, in obedience, in truth.

Walking in holiness means to live a life marked by a distinct separateness. We like fitting in, but holiness requires that we set ourselves apart from the rest of the world for God's service. It's not that we have to live as hermits, but out attitudes and reactions should be different from the culture around us.

Walking in obedience means that we know and commit to following God's precepts as a habit, as a practice. We don't and choose which instructions to follow, we diligently seek to honor God in everything we do.

Walking in truth means we recognize Jesus redeemed us completely, not because we deserved but because He loves us. We don't have to perform to earn His favor and we have the privilege of sharing that with others.

In addition, walking in the light keeps me safe from the effects of sin, and protects me from hurts that might slow me down or put me out of the race for a time.

It's a dark world out there. Stay in the light.

What is the most difficult part of walking in the light—holiness, obedience or truth?

7

Taking Breaks

And He said to them, "Come aside by yourselves to a deserted place and rest a while." For there were many coming and going, and they did not even have time to eat.
Mark 6:31

Some days, I sleep in. I don't run every day. I have planned days off. Some days, I don't even run the whole distance—I'll take a break every mile or mile and half and walk for a bit. It sounds counterintuitive, but the breaks actually help my strength and endurance more than running all out all the time.

I take a day off after a long run, or after several days of average runs in a row. But I've also taken days off when I'm extra tired and could use the extra hour of sleep. (I try not to take advantage of that one.) I don't skip a day after a bad outing, though.

I need occasional breaks in my Christian race as well. Now I'm not suggesting taking a break FROM your faith and living like a heathen in order to strengthen your commitment, but we do need breaks from ministry from time to time. Jesus modeled this for us in the gospels. When do we need breaks?

Routine scheduled breaks - Luke 5:16 tells us that Jesus often withdrew to the wilderness to pray, and recharge. In a careful reading of the rest of Luke's gospel, you'll catch Jesus taking these timeouts frequently. Plan to go to Bible study rather than teach once in a while, or visit a different church. You might even attend a retreat or conference. The key is planning for it and not waiting for it to develop. *Look at your calendar—when can you take a break?*

After success – When the Twelve returned from a preaching and healing tour of Galilee, flush with success, Jesus immediately took them aside to a desert place to decompress. We tend to think you need to immediately build on success to perpetuate it. The break helps us remember the One who engineered the success, and our dependence on Him.

But not after failure - After Peter's denial, he'd given up on his ministry. He was sure he'd blown his opportunity and headed back to the fishing business. In John 20:15-22, Jesus reaffirms his call and encourages Peter to get back to work. When we experience a setback, our reflex is to quit. We question the path we're on, and God who put us there. That easily leads to completely abandoning our mission.

Before burnout - Just as your body can't function properly without adequate rest, we can't minister if our own well is dry. It's not selfish to take a day or a season off to recharge.
Don't stop, but rest.

Why do we find it so difficult to take breaks? Does the influence of our fast-paced culture keep us from slowing down? Do you have a method for balancing ministry and personal renewal?

8

Surprising Results

And Elisha prayed, and said, "LORD, I pray, open his eyes that he may see." Then the LORD opened the eyes of the young man, and he saw. And behold, the mountain was full of horses and chariots of fire all around Elisha. 2 Kings 6:17

The primary reason I started running was to lose weight. Women who reach ... a certain age ... often take their fat cells (many times joined with a few more) with them to the grave. Unless something drastic changes it.

Additionally, I had gestational diabetes with my son, bumping me into a higher risk group for developing Type II diabetes. Keeping my weight in line keeps me from jumping yet another notch higher on that risk scale.

For the first two years, **I lost exactly ZERO pounds**. None. Sigh.

But I was shocked when I had some bloodwork done. In that same timeframe, **my cholesterol dropped 21 points**. I wasn't even working on that.

What does this have to do with running your race? Often God works with us in areas we don't expect, don't realize, and He brings about results that glorify Him we never imagined.

- You pray for a family member for years, but nothing happens. Except your kids see what persevering faith is.
- You teach a roomful of kids in Sunday school or VBS, and see no growth. Except 20 years later, a young adult comes back to church, and changes the course of his family's life.
- You go sit in worship services week after week and feel like you don't contribute. Except the preacher knows he can count on you to be there.

So, don't measure your progress on some limited, temporary number. God measures results on an eternal, multidimensional scale. He says even a cup of water given in His name won't go unnoticed.

Keep running. Great things are happening.

Why are results so important to us? Pride? Insecurity? Have you ever been surprised by your efforts in your walk of faith? Does that encourage you when you don't see results?

9

No Winter Break

And whoever does not bear his cross and come after Me cannot be My disciple. Luke 14:27

One fall the cold weather came early. Even before it was officially winter, the morning temps plunged below my comfort zone. Around here, it happened suddenly. Thirty-seven one morning. Twenty-three the next. And then it got colder.

On the long-range forecast, there were a couple of days that might warm up enough, but that was a big maybe. Even if it did warm up, it would only be for a day or two, and January was still looming. I was stuck.

Now, I may say I'm not running in the rain, or when it gets below thirty degrees, but things are different running that race that God has called me to. **Following Him, there are no arbitrary limits set according to my comfort or preferences.** I don't tell God, "I'll follow you today, but not on Saturdays." Or "I'll believe what You say about my salvation, but not about my obligations to be obedient." I don't get to pick which eight out of ten commandments I want to keep.

Following Jesus Christ, **running the race He sets before me is a 24/7 lifetime pursuit.** The weather, the season of life, the circumstances don't change the fact that because Jesus saved my soul, He owns me. He is Lord. He decides, and I run.

What areas of your life do you struggle turning over to Jesus? Why is it difficult to surrender everything to Him? Trust? Control? A misunderstanding of the word 'Lord'? Has He ever disappointed you as you followed Him?

1 0

False Standards

For I say to you, that unless your righteousness exceeds the righteousness of the scribes and Pharisees, you will by no means enter the kingdom of heaven. Matthew 5:20

One weekend when we had traveled to visit family, I packed my running gear and made plans to run. My husband always packs his, but instead of doing his usual thirteen mile torture circuit, he consented to run with me just for fun. Now, Jon runs much faster and much farther than I do, but he's twitterpated, so off we went.

My gear included a watch with a countdown timer and a cheap pedometer. My husband, the more serious runner, was given one of those high-tech, chest-strap, GPS, heart-rate, instantaneous speed, NASA, Olympic watches. It's the type of thing he would never spend money on, but he kind of likes it.

My goal for the day was to run eighteen minutes then walk a bit, then run two ten-minute cycles and hopefully that would be three and a half miles or so. At the end of the eighteen minutes, I pulled my pedometer off and it registered 1.9 miles. Not bad. My first year, it was September before I could run two miles straight. This was May. And my pace was right around 9.5 minutes a mile. Then Jon announced "That's 1.6 miles."

What? "Yeah, 1.6 miles." Hmmm… That's an 11.25 mile pace. I wasn't running nearly as fast or as far as I thought. My pedometer was off. Even though I much preferred my results, **they were measured against a false standard**.

It's easy to measure our walk, our lives, against the false standard of the world around us. Compared to "those" people, we're doing well. However, **when we hold our lives up against the standards God reveals in His word, the results are quite different.** When Isaiah was shown a vision of God's holiness, the ultimate standard, his reaction was, *"It's all over! I am doomed!"* (NLT)

Measuring ourselves against God's standard we see how desperately we need His great mercy and His super-abundant grace.

Why is it critical to have an accurate view of ourselves and our standing before God? What problems can results if we use a false standard?

11

Preventing Chafing

Then He answered and spoke to those who stood before Him, saying, "Take away the filthy garments from him." And to him He said, "See, I have removed your iniquity from you, and I will clothe you with rich robes." Zechariah 3:4

I hadn't run very long before I got chafed. I'm not sure if that's a good milestone or a bad one, but it is a memorable one. The sting will transform that relaxing, post-run shower into a prying-yourself-from-the-ceiling moment. (Or worse, depending on where you happen to get chafed.)

It is almost solely a result of wearing the wrong type of clothing. Like cotton. I love cotton, but it quickly gets wet and having that wet clothing rubbing against you for a few miles is the easiest recipe for chafing.

Living around other folks we're bound to get chafed, too. With some people, it's their superpower, rubbing you the wrong way with everything they say or do. Just like with running, the key to preventing chafing is carefully choosing what you put on. After a search of the New Testament, I found these:

*"For as many of you as were baptized into Christ have put on **Christ**."* Galatians 3:27

*"...put on **the new man** which was created according to God, in true righteousness and holiness."* Ephesians 4:24

"Therefore, as the elect of God, holy and beloved, put on **tender mercies, kindness, humility, meekness, longsuffering"** Colossians 3:12

*"But above all these things put on **love**, which is the bond of perfection."* Colossians 3:14

Christ, the new man, tender mercies, kindness, humility, meekness, longsuffering and love. See if those don't cut down on chafing.

Usually garments are a symbol of our righteousness in Christ. What's different about the analogy here? How critical is preparation when faced with difficult people or situations?

12

Sidelined

My flesh and my heart may fail, but God is the strength of my heart and my portion forever. Psalm 73:26 NAS

The muscles behind my knee let me know I'd overextended them. Maybe I have an inherent weakness. Maybe I didn't properly prepare. Maybe I took a wrong step.

The thing is, I didn't realize I'd pulled those muscles while I was running. It wasn't until later that evening, when it hurt to walk or come down the stairs that I knew. This isn't the first time, either. Those muscles have sidelined me even during the winter when I'm not running.

So instead of hitting the pavement, I got busy with the ice pack, ibuprofen and stretching, trying to heal quickly and prevent any further damage.

I have weak spots in my Christian life as well—attitudes and insecurities that make me vulnerable.

Sometimes I'm not just poorly prepared. I rush into things on my own strength.

Or maybe, subtle attitude shifts often lead to a wrong step.

Then I realize I don't feel like running anymore.

When that happens, I need extra study time, more prayer, and active, intentional worship to get me going again. I have to be intentional about each one of those or I'll be sidelined even longer.

As you run your race for Christ, are you aware of your weak spots? Do you know what might sideline you? How do you get back in the race?

13

Discipling

[God] comforts us in all our troubles so that we can comfort others. When they are troubled, we will be able to give them the same comfort God has given us. 1 Corinthians 1:4 (NLT)

After a week of normal running and super aerobic VBS music, my knee seemed to be ready for me to resume my plan to hit five miles (continuous) before the season is out.

With football season right around the corner, my son has been getting up and running my last mile with me. For a time, my daughter ran with me, but she's decided she's more of an afternoon runner. Even so, it's fun to have a buddy, and it's fun to coach my kids along.

On the flip side, every once in a while, I'll run with my husband, he of the "eight-and-a-half-minute-mile, eleven mile" runs. Thankfully, he lets me set the pace and I feel accomplished just getting out with him.

Even on my solo runs, he encourages me, and checks on my progress. He's good to diagnose my pains and recommend treatment. If we need more help, we consult with his running buddy, Jay.

In the same way that I'm coaching and being coached as a runner, as believers, we find ourselves in between newer and more mature Christians, with opportunities to learn and to teach. The New Testament is full of descriptions on how this works in the body of Christ. My favorite is 2 Corinthians 1:4.

It clearly explains that all the lessons we learn in our trials, all the comfort we receive, God expects us to turn around and share that with someone else.

See, He designed the coaching system.

Who are you coaching, encouraging, mentoring or discipling?
Who do you look to for advice or inspiration?

14

Attacked While Running

Stay alert! Watch out for your great enemy, the devil. He prowls around like a roaring lion, looking for someone to devour. 1 Peter 5:8 NLT

I'm typically cautious when I run. I don't use headphones so I can hear everything around me. I make sure I'm visible. I carry my cell phone, and I really watch the pavement for uneven spots.

One morning I headed out, ready to conquer my southern route. Early out the road dips down toward a creek between the grade school and a wooded park. It's nice to get that hill out of the way at the beginning of the run.

I had run the downhill side and was just about to start up when I got hit on the top of my head! My first thought was that it was a bat—a fat, clumsy bat, maybe. I didn't see anything though.

I hoped it wasn't somebody in the woods throwing rocks at me. Finally, I decided it was something from the trees, a piece of bark or something that seemed bigger than it was because it surprised me. Okay. Whew.

Then it happened again!

And this time I saw it. An owl. A good-sized owl had thumped me. (I say 'thumped,' because there were no talons involved. Thankfully!)

After a little investigation, we found out she's a barn owl, and a regular 'thump-er.' At least three other runners have encountered her. The Department of Natural Resources told us that in a few weeks—maybe when her babies are bigger, or gone—she won't be as aggressive. Even so, I changed my route. Just to be safe.

So what's the lesson?

1. Even if you think you're cautious and well-prepared, **attacks can come from the most unexpected places and using the most unexpected means**. I've seen plenty of deer, dogs and even one skunk on my morning runs, but it was the owl that got me. We can be prayed up, studied up, tight with God and that doesn't exempt us. Don't be surprised or dismayed.

2. **Keep running**. Granted, I checked more than once to make sure I was just sweating and not bleeding, and I was really jumpy for the rest of the run, but I kept going. I ended up making both my marks for distance. I didn't let the attack prevent me from reaching my goal.

Can you recall a time when you were attacked, maybe even unexpectedly? What was the key to getting yourself back in the race?

15

To the Fullest

The thief does not come except to steal, and to kill, and to destroy. I have come that they may have life, and that they may have it more abundantly. John 10:10

My first 5K was a nice easy race in the town where I live. I didn't quite think I was ready, but after some persuasion from a friend, there I was. I had three goals:

- Don't get lost.
- Don't lose my keys.
- Finish in under thirty-six minutes. (That's a little under a twelve-minute-mile pace. Not very fast.)

I met my goals. Maybe the reason I met them is they weren't especially audacious. I was number eighty-two out of one hundred seventy-one. Runners and non-runners alike were very supportive and encouraging. 'You ran a race—that alone was a great thing,' they said.

Truth be known, I should have been able to finish in under thirty-three minutes based on my times from this past summer. With training, effort and commitment, twenty-seven minutes isn't impossible. But then again, maybe it is. Thirty to thirty-three minutes sounds better to me. **Doable, but not too taxing.**

The thing is, **that complacency invades the rest of my life, especially my spiritual life.** I tend to settle for a life that qualifies as Christian, but doesn't require much effort or investment. I get satisfied with showing up and going through the motions.

In John 10:10, Jesus says, *"I have come that they may have life, and that they may have it more abundantly."* More abundantly. In the Greek, that's beyond abundant, superabundant even, or superior (in quality), exceedingly, beyond measure. **Life to the fullest.**

It's silly for me to settle for a Christian walk that's just "doable" when Christ has so much more for me. The best part about it—the hard work has already been done.

Are you choosing a doable or a superabundant life? Why do you suppose people prefer an easier, manageable walk than the superabundant one Christ intended?

16

Running with a Beginner

You therefore, my son, be strong in the grace that is in Christ Jesus. 2 Timothy 2:1

When my son was eleven, he signed up for his first race, a two-miler. I promised my son I'd run with him since it was his first race, and we officially registered. Honestly, I think he was mostly in it for the shirt. Oh, and lunch afterwards.

My husband ran a ten-mile race as part of the same event. **It would be unfair and even a little cruel to expect Alan run the ten-mile race his first time out.** Two miles is much better suited to his abilities (and mine). However, many times we expect new believers to behave the way veteran Christians do.

Rather than saddle them with more than they're ready for, let's come alongside and run with them. Help them maintain their pace. Point out their progress and encourage them to keep going.

If I don't prepare adequately I can't help my son at all. It means getting up when the alarm goes off. Some days that means shifting my running time a little later in the day (when it's warmer) to ensure that I get my run in. More running means more laundry. But my son's counting on me. I can't let him down.

I'm not sure we grasp how much newer believers depend on us. We have to shift our routines around for their sakes. If they see us giving up, laying down or sleeping in, they will too.

Having both races the same day, **it will be tempting to look at the ten-milers and feel completely inadequate**, especially since a number of them will run the two-mile as a warm-up for their race. Sheesh. The thing is, the two-milers get the same refreshments and the same shirt as the ten-milers.

God lays a different race before each of us, and it's the one suited to our abilities and preparation. We shouldn't feel inferior to believers who have appear to have more faith, or more knowledge or some incredible ministry. At the end, we all get the same shirt—the righteousness of Christ.

How do you encourage folks who haven't been believers as long as you have? What encouragement have you received?

1 7

Better Than Expected

His lord said to him, 'Well done, good and faithful servant; you were faithful over a few things, I will make you ruler over many things. Enter into the joy of your lord.' Matthew 25:21

So, that two-mile race I ran with my son . . . It was 30 degrees and snowing when we left the house. By race time, there was a stiff, cutting wind quickly followed by snow and ice pellets.

I had a terrible race. I have trouble running in cold weather so I never venture out when it's below thirty. Plus I NEVER run in precipitation. Never.

I had hoped to finish in twenty-two minutes or less, and I hit that in my practice runs. On race day, I was two ticks over twenty-three minutes. But with the conditions, I was okay with that. My son finished in 20:50, a great run his first time out and in adverse conditions. We gave ourselves bonus points for finishing and called it a day.

Here's the crazy thing.

We found out later . . . **I won my age division.** I thought that race was one of my worst outings ever, but I wasn't the scorekeeper. The scorekeeper said I won.

When we run our race as believers, **it's easy to get discouraged.** We run against circumstances we can't control. Often the race is more challenging than we anticipated, and our own unmet expectations can make us hard-pressed to keep going.

But the scorekeeper, **Jesus Christ, has a much truer clearer picture of our race.** Not only that, we can be confident He's not going to judge us against other believers (you know the type—like the seventeen-year-old boys who run 5-minute miles).

The key to winning my race was **signing up, showing up to run, and finishing**. For us as believers, it's not much different. We trust Jesus and we live that out every day. I think once we finish, we will be astounded by how well we did.

How is knowing Jesus is the scorekeeper an encouragement? In what ways do you think His scoring system might differ from ours?

1 8

Marathon Training

Then the King will say to those on His right hand,
'Come, you blessed of My Father, inherit the kingdom
prepared for you from the foundation of the world:
Matthew 25:34

One summer, I happened to catch the results for L.A. Marathon. The winner finished in 2 hours and 12 minutes. That's a mile every 5 minutes. My long run so far this season was 4.25 miles. A marathon is six times that distance. And the winner ran over twice as fast as I do.

If I wanted to run a marathon . . . I'd have to make some major lifestyle changes.

My schedule would have to shift to accommodate running up to four hours a day.

My priorities would be rearranged with running near the top.

My diet would change.

I'd need some gear.

I'd need another pair of shoes because I'd wear out my current ones in training (which is sad because they are brand new and I really like them).

And I'd need a mentor, someone with experience running marathons who could set up a training schedule for me and make sure I stick to it.

Now I guarantee if I took that on, there would be pain, exhaustion and discomfort. I would have to be dedicated, committed and goal-oriented. Above all, I'd have to listen to my mentor. You see where I'm going with this.

But it struck me today—**this life is not the main event**. Paul talks about running our race, and we're in the middle of a book about the things I've learned since I started running. But this is all training. The things we go through in this life are prepping us for eternity. The marathon is still ahead.

Keeping that in mind, I need to evaluate how I'm doing. As I train . . .

- Have I made the necessary changes to my life? This must be my priority.
- Am I giving my full effort? I have to run every mile.
- Am I listening to my mentor, Jesus Christ, and following the program He's designed for me?

What about you? How is your training coming along? How does knowing eternity is the ultimate goal change your perspective?

19

Running with Endurance

"...[L]et us run with endurance the race that is set before us" Hebrews 12:1

There was one particular morning, a Monday, when I ran farther than I had ever run before—nearly 7 miles. I left the house a little after 5 a.m. and got home around 6:15. I ran the whole time. Seventy-two minutes. (I'm pretty slow.) Not only that, but it was my third straight "longest ever." I wasn't doing anything different than what I did the summer before that when I couldn't break 5.5 miles. Well, maybe there was one thing different—I was learning the mental side to running. I was learning my body can do more than I realize if I don't give in to its whining. I was also learning to listen to my internal "coach" and not the "critic."

Of course, all this has a spiritual application. We can do far more for the cause of Christ than we realize ("all things," the apostle Paul said in Philippians 4:13). However, it is all too easy to listen to that voice inside.

You know, the one that says, *"That will never work."* Or, *"You're not qualified."* Or, *"You're just one person. You'll never make a difference."*

How would things change if we listened to our Holy Spirit "coach" instead? What would our families and churches and neighborhoods be like if we grabbed hold of, *"You have everything you need. You've got this."* Or, *"That discomfort is because you're doing something. Keep going!"* Or *"Look how far you've gone!"*

When God called us, He equipped us. We can do the ministry He's given us to do. We absolutely can. He has infused us with the Holy Spirit, the same one from Pentecost. But we have to make the effort and we have to endure.

A side note: Endure doesn't mean "exhaust yourself." Sometimes we have to make sure we are running the race God has laid out and not running extra miles someone else piles on us.

Bottom line- Don't quit. Hang on and push through, and you'll start to see amazing things happen.

How hard is it to ignore your inner critic? What is the single biggest encouragement you've heard? Who needs to hear that same kind of encouragement today from you?

20

Trainer or Racer?

According to my earnest expectation and hope that in nothing I shall be ashamed, but with all boldness, as always, so now also Christ will be magnified in my body, whether by life or by death. Philippians 1:20

My fourth race was a Memorial Day 5K. Here's what I learned: **I'm terrible at races**. I took a month of great training runs, of shaving seconds off my time, and translated that into my worst 5K time to date.

It was tempting to blame the heat. (It was about 20-25 degrees warmer than training temps.) Or the hill. (The half mile between 1.5 and 2. Ugh.) Or the crowded race field. (I'm used to running alone.)

I was frustrated enough that I considered scrapping plans for a series of races—a 10K, 15K and half marathon—that fall. Adding to the aggravation, my husband conquered his first triathlon two days before the Memorial Day race, then sailed through the 5K.

But here's what concerns me more. I'm the same way in my Christian life. I'm great at training—at studying my Bible every morning, attending church services and so forth. But when it comes to testing those things, to putting theory into practice, I often choke.

So how do I fix this?

I keep training. I'll never run a successful race without good training. And that was the part I did fairly well at. That goes for my walk too. I need to keep up those spiritual disciplines—study, prayer, worship—if I have any hope of running well.

I keep running races. I have to keep putting myself to the test, signing up for the fall races. Spiritually, the same thing applies. I have to allow God to put me in situations where I have to use what I've learned, even when it pulls me beyond what's comfortable.

I keep striving. Personal bests are never permanent. (Sadly, personal 'worsts' may not be either.) I'll have a breakthrough one of these days, as long as I keep putting on my sneakers. As a believer, Hebrews 12 tells me to run with endurance. After all, those folks in chapter 11 did, and look where it got them.

What about you? Are you better at "training," or "racing,"? How can we become bolder as believers?

2 1

After an Injury

*Therefore, strengthen the hands that are weak and
the knees that are feeble, and make straight paths for
your feet, so that the limb which is lame may not be
put out of joint, but rather be healed. Hebrews 12:12-
13 NAS*

I had a great plan for the running season one year. I
wanted to hit 10K, but I didn't make it. The next year I
made that distance in April. *April.* So I set my sights on a
half marathon by fall. I found a series of races—a 10K in
August, a 15K in September and a half-marathon in
October. Perfect.

Then knee pain hit and everything unraveled. I got really
discouraged. I'm a goal-oriented type and scrapping my
race plans was a major failure. I couldn't run three-quarters
of a mile without serious pain. I had trouble walking
without pain. And steps? Forget it.

I took two weeks off—it still hurt. I got a knee brace—it
still hurt. I iced and wrapped and stretched . . . it still hurt.

Finally, it was decision time. I could work through the pain and keep running OR conclude running wasn't my thing after all.

I decided to run. Somehow or other.

I consulted with an experienced runner. He gave me a set of exercises and an admonition to run on the track. So I did. The plan was running a half mile, stretching, walking, then running another half mile. I worked up to two miles, then two and a half, then running a mile at a time. Little by little. Eventually I got back up to three miles, and running on consecutive days.

So what does my whining have to do with anything?

Running the race God sets before us is not always easy and **sometimes we encounter pain and difficulty**. It could be anything from opposition and conflict to church politics to failures to . . . you name it. When something like that happens, we don't stop running altogether but we do need to take care of ourselves. How do we do that?

I had to leave my schedule and plan, and go back to the basics. Sometimes when we serve Christ, we get so busy ministering, we lose sight of the One we're trying to serve. We get ideas, we jump into to programs, and we go ninety miles an hour, nonstop. Until we get hurt. Discouraged. Defeated. When that happens, we need to take a break and refocus on the basics of who Christ is and who we are in Him.

I had to strengthen my knees. BUT that only happened when I worked on my hips. Turns out the tendons from my hip muscles were pulling my knees. The exercises my friend recommended were for my hips. Be ready to strengthen the weak areas in your Christian life but always be aware—they may not be where you think they are. You may need a wise coach to help you diagnose the source.

I switched to the track while I healed. We may need to switch to a "softer" area of service for a bit to recover and revive. It's a way to prevent long-term damage or ministry burn-out.

I'm making progress. Each day I run a little longer, and my knee hurts a little less, and recovers from the day's run a little sooner. I hope to be back on schedule before the season ends. When we get back into running our race for Christ after pain and difficulty, look for progress—strengthening, more endurance, and quicker recovery from routine stresses—and be encouraged by that.

Have you ever had to quit running for a while (physically or spiritually)? What helped you recover?

2 2

Mentoring While We Run

For I have passed on to them the message you gave me. They accepted it and know that I came from you, and they believe you sent me. John 17:8 NLT

Not too long ago, my daughter was flirting with the idea of running some challenging fall races. She likes the idea of running, but the doing . . . not so much. As she was preparing to head out one afternoon, I overheard her brother coaching her. "It will probably hurt, maybe the whole time, but you have to keep going. That's how you get stronger."

Good advice. It made me smile for a couple of reasons. One, he's younger and rarely gets to coach her on anything. Second, I had said very similar words to him one morning not too long ago when his leg muscles were rebelling.

In my experience, runners are extremely helpful with advice and tips for those of us who haven't been lacing the shoes quite as long. I rely on my husband and his buddy,

Jay, and a few online coaches. But I also do my best to encourage my kids, offering to train with them or race with them.

My son was in a unique "in-between" spot as a runner, both coaching but still being coached. Our Christian walk is marked by the same balance, as we are constantly learning and sharing, teaching and mentoring in the body of Christ. Consider these three benefits.

It strengthens the bond between us. Think back through the challenging times in your life. Do you feel a connection to those who counseled you or walked through those times with you? Or maybe there was a time when you were there for a friend or family member.

It encourages both people. New Testament writers Paul and John both mentioned the joy that came with hearing the new believers were standing firm, taking their teaching to heart and living out the truth. It's a real blessing to have someone invest themselves in you.

It models Christ. In the beautiful prayer recorded in John 17, Jesus mentions several things He received from the Father that He, in turn, gave to His followers. So we should freely give all the encouragement and insight we've received.

Who are you mentoring right now? Who is mentoring you? Can you think of a past mentor you are especially indebted to? Why not let them know how much his or her influence meant?

23

Reflecting

> *Do all things without grumbling or questioning, that you may be blameless and innocent, children of God without blemish in the midst of a crooked and twisted generation,* **among whom you shine as lights in the world**, *holding fast to the word of life, so that in the day of Christ I may be proud that I did not run in vain or labor in vain. Philippians 2:14-16 ESV*

Except for a few weeks in the summer, it's dark when I run. In the early spring and late fall, it's dark the entire time I'm out, so for safety's sake, my reflective vest is required equipment. I used to rely on white shirts, and as long as I'm on the track or at the park, I guess those are adequate. But out on the road I need something better.

In the same way, running our Christian race, **we run in a really dark world and it's critical that we reflect Jesus**. Oh sure, in the safety of our churches and our circle of friends, we might be able to get by with just our white shirts. On the dark streets, though, the reflected light shines brighter than any shirt ever could.

These verses in Philippians point to one way we can reflect Christ—our attitude. Our world is full of grumbling and complaining about everything from the latest government policies to the way our snacks are packaged. The house is cold. There is nothing to watch on television. My gum doesn't keep its flavor long enough. I have too much to do. I don't get enough rest, and on and on.

Making just this one change—not grumbling and complaining—will be a noticeable bright spot in our increasingly dark culture.

Does your attitude reflect Christ? What other ways do you reflect Him? What way or in what situation is it most difficult to reflect Him?

2 4

Run, Don't Perform

"Are you tired? Worn out? Burned out on religion? Come to me. Get away with me and you'll recover your life. I'll show you how to take a real rest. Walk with me and work with me—watch how I do it. Learn the unforced rhythms of grace. I won't lay anything heavy or ill-fitting on you. Keep company with me and you'll learn to live freely and lightly." Matthew *11:28-30,* The Message

I'm better runner than racer, which isn't saying much, but it is what it is. One month, after carefully stretching and babying my knee, I signed up for a 5K. My previous best had been 35:19.

For this race, my goal was to finish in under 35 minutes. Nothing too dramatic, but it would mean pushing my knee just a bit. So the night before the race I did the math and knew I needed to run better than 11:17 each mile to meet that goal.

Race day came and off we went. At mile 1, I checked my watch. Twelve minutes. Twelve. I would have to run well under eleven minutes for the next two miles to hit my goal. That was too fast. Crud.

It was tempting . . . really tempting . . .to get monumentally discouraged at that point, and quit trying. My knee hurt. That's a legitimate reason (excuse) for a poor outing, right? But my son was running. And my husband. So I took a big, deep breath and decided my new goal was to finish without walking, a good enough goal for the bad knee. The pressure was off. I ran relaxed.

Here's the thing. I finished the whole race in under 34 minutes. Almost a minute and a half faster than my best outing. My last two miles were under 10:30. I never run that fast. Never.

So what happened?

I stopped worrying about my **performance** and concentrated on **finishing**. I stopped **measuring myself** against external metrics and **just ran the race** laid out before me.

You can see the application, can't you? So many times I get caught up meeting artificial goals or performance indicators that I forget to just run. When I look around and decide where I should be in my Christian life at a given time and I don't make that, I get really discouraged.

Jesus never put those demands on me. He never calls on me to compare myself to others or to a man-made standard.

The idea of performing or measuring to win or keep God's favor is contrary to the reality of His grace. Because Jesus Christ shed His blood on my behalf, I can run relaxed. The pressure's off. The victory is won. I just have to run the race laid out in front of me.

In what areas of your life are you most tempted to fall into performing rather than just running? Why is it so difficult for us to embrace the reality of grace?

2 5

A Kids' Race

Bear one another's burdens, and so fulfill the law of Christ. Galatians 6:2

When my youngest ran her first race, she and the rest of the kids discovered they each had a personalized sign on the race route to urge them on.

The course was two laps around the block. It may not sound like much, but for legs that short, it's a long way. I mean, after you make it all the way around the block... you have to do it again!

Even with the signs, there were more than a handful of little ones with red faces ready to call it a day after that first lap. However, the crowd cheered like crazy. Moms and dads knifed through the spectators, took their little ones by the hand and said, "Come on. You can do this. One more lap. I'll go with you."

So they kept running. No matter how wobbly things looked there in the middle, when the announcer called their names, and they came across the finish line, the kids beamed.

Isn't that the way our Christian race is supposed to work?

- Finishing is the goal.
- Everybody cheering and encouraging you to keep going.
- Folks stepping out to run alongside you.
- No matter how tough things are in the middle, it will be worth it to hear our names called at the finish line.

Unfortunately, it doesn't always happen that way. We get consumed by competing, by our performance and we lose the joy. We get heckled instead of encouraged. We run alone. Sometimes we even give up.

Remember what it says in Hebrews 12:1-2?

*Therefore we also, since we are surrounded by so great a cloud of witnesses, let us lay aside every weight, and the sin which so easily ensnares us, and **let us run** with endurance the race that is set before us, looking unto Jesus, the author and finisher of our faith, who **for the joy** that was set before Him endured the cross, despising the shame, and has sat down at the right hand of the throne of God.*

Don't give up. Keep the finish line in mind and run that next lap. You can do this. I'm running with you.

How does knowing you're not alone encourage you? Can you think of a time you wished someone had come alongside you? Were there opportunities to run with someone else that you have missed? Why do you think Jesus wants us to help each other out this way?

26

Imitating Runners

Imitate me, just as I also imitate Christ. 1 Corinthians 11:1

One icy January Saturday, my husband, two of his running buddies, and my son took off to run the Polar Bear Dare. It's a 10K trail run—up hill, down hill, in the mud, through thigh deep water, and repeat for an hour and a half or so. It was physically strenuous, mentally taxing . . . and really muddy. My husband threw his shoes away after it was over.

My son ran a one-mile event, but after hanging out with the guys, he said he wanted to run the 10K next year. He knows what the race is like, but something about Jon, Jay and Bobby and the other runners made him want to run the way they do.

I think that's an amazing compliment.

Now let's apply it to our lives as believers. Paul says in 1 Corinthians 11:1 *"Imitate me, just as I also imitate Christ."*

Do you know someone who has a faith that inspires you? Maybe it's someone who has faced the same kind of trials you have. Maybe it's someone who makes you want to run like they do.

The flip side is more challenging. Do we encourage others to **persevere**, to **step out in faith**, to **try hard things** just by the way we live our lives? Does anyone look at us and say, "I want to run like she does, or like he does?" If not, now's your chance!

Good luck and watch out for the mud!

Who do you imitate? What specific ways do they point you to Christ? Who imitates you? What do they see in you that reflects Christ? (Be objective about this. What people imitate is an indication of where your gifts are.)

2 7

Eyes on the Prize

Do you not know that those who run in a race all run, but one receives the prize? Run in such a way that you may obtain it. 1 Corinthians 9:24

Some days it's hard to get up and run. I mean really hard. Like that Monday. I was still recovering from the time change and there was precipitation, almost enough to be classified as a drizzle. (I don't run in the rain.) **But I had a race in two weeks.** So I ran, and I made my race distance.

Then came Tuesday. The temperature dropped down into the thirties. The bed was warm. I was tired. I could take Tuesday as my day off instead of Wednesday . . . **But I have a race in two weeks.** So I got up and ran the race distance again, a little faster.

I guarantee you, if there had not been a race coming up, I would have reset my alarm and gone back to sleep.

The goal, the prize changes everything.

Paul says in 1 Corinthians, *"Don't you realize that in a race everyone runs, but only one person gets the prize? So run to win! All athletes are disciplined in their training. They do it to win a prize that will fade away,* **but we do it for an eternal prize.** *So I run with purpose in every step."* (9:24-26a, NLT).

It's so easy to lose sight of that prize and focus on the immediate things around us. It doesn't seem to matter if they are comforts (like a warm bed) or challenges (It's raining and I'm tired), they are equally distracting.

However, when we focus on the goal, the prize, the eternal prize, we are much more likely to keep running.

What things are most likely to get you to take your eyes off the prize? What helps you refocus?

2 8

Running and Following For Real

Then He said to the crowd, "If any of you wants to be my follower, you must turn from your selfish ways, take up your cross daily, and follow Me." Luke 9:23 NLT

I could talk about running all day long, but that's not what makes me a runner.

My lightweight stability sneakers, my moisture-wicking shirts, my knee brace and my high-tech GPS watch don't go together to make me a runner.

Hanging out with runners, reading articles, learning the jargon and liking a bunch of running pages on Facebook won't make me a runner either.

The only thing that will make me a runner is . . . running.

In the same way, I can say I'm a follower of Jesus all day long.

I can use the catch-phrases. I can hang out with other followers. I can read all the right books, attend conferences, wear t-shirts, and put decals on my car, but none of that makes me a follower of Jesus.

The thing that makes me a follower of Jesus is . . . following.
His commands. His teaching. His example.

What are some elements of Christian "culture" that don't have much to do with following Jesus? Why do you think we readily embrace the trappings of Christianity, but shy away from the commitment?

2 9

Running on the Beach

Jesus said to him, "If I will that he remain till I come, what is that to you? You follow Me." John 21:22

One morning while we were vacationing in Panama City, Jon and I got up early to go for a run on the beach. He was still recovering from a stress fracture so my speed and distance suited him just fine. Off we went. Barefoot. In the sand.

Here's what I know about running on the beach. It. Is. Hard. My calves hurt for three days.

But there was something else I noticed, too. On the sand, you leave an unmistakable set of footprints. Your stride length and how you orient your toes are obvious. And in the wet sand, the impressions are deep.

That morning, there were a few spots where, because of the way the sand banked and the how the tide was coming in, I was forced to run in Jon's tracks. It was nearly impossible. He takes two steps to my three or three and a half. His foot is bigger. He turns his feet out more. It was awful. I had to slow down even more, and watch my feet to keep from stumbling or turning an ankle. I did much better when I could make my own tracks.

I think we run into to similar problems in our Christian race when we try to run in another believer's tracks. This doesn't mean we shouldn't have mentors, or examples, because we absolutely should. However, we also need to recognize and remember that God calls us as individuals, each with a unique role to play in His kingdom work.

In the last chapter of John's gospel, Peter has a brief but intense conversation with Jesus about his future. Jesus doesn't soften the details, but Peter is still committed. In verses 20-21 though, *"Peter, turning around, saw the disciple whom Jesus loved following them ... So Peter seeing him said to Jesus, "Lord, and what about this man?""*

See, even when we have a clear idea of our purpose, our mission, our calling, it's easy to look around, see how someone else is running and begin to question things.

Maybe I should be doing what they're doing. Maybe their tracks are the right tracks. Maybe I should be running in their tracks. It's especially tempting if someone else has more perceived success than we do.

However, Jesus said in verse 22, *"If I want him to remain until I come, what is that to you? You follow Me!"*

Don't worry about John. Just be Peter, and do what I have for you to do. In a way, Jesus said, "Run in your own tracks."

Where is your race taking you? What tempts you to slide over into another set of tracks?

3 0

Overtaken

And all these blessings shall come upon you and overtake you, because you obey the voice of the LORD your God: Deuteronomy 28:2

Even weak links get medals

For one race, I got to be the weak link on a triathlon team, thanks to my husband's still-healing stress fracture. Jon did the hard parts, the swimming and the biking, and my job was to run the 5K.

Because Jon is a strong swimmer, and the race used a delayed start, I got to take off on the run portion smack in the middle of the top athletes. For a brief moment, I was ahead of some of the fastest runners in the community. In fact, I wish I had pictures of myself . . . leading . . . Then reality set in, and I think seven or ten of them passed me before I finished.

Each time, it happened the same way. I heard the footfalls behind me. Then came the sense that someone was close. This was followed by a momentary delusion that maybe I could speed up and stay ahead. Of course, this yielded to the inevitable. "Good job," they said as they passed, and they meant it. Speedy runners are a nice bunch.

In Deuteronomy 28, Moses is winding down his last instructions and admonitions for the nation of Israel and in verse 2, he says, *"And all these blessings shall come upon you and overtake you, because you obey the voice of the Lord your God."*

I like that image. God always blesses obedience, but He doesn't just throw blessings out there and if we're lucky we'll run into them. No, He makes sure they catch us.

Think of it. All these blessings, He said.

We can't outrun them or get away from them. He promises they will overtake us.

How do you usually think about God's blessings? As random events? As rare occurrences? As entitlements? Something else? What does our view of God's blessings say about our view of God Himself?

Trust the Training

And my speech and my preaching were not with persuasive words of human wisdom, but in demonstration of the Spirit and of power, that your faith should not be in the wisdom of men but in the power of God. 1 Corinthians 2:4-5

I have a confession . . . The truth is, I'm a sissy. I don't run when it's cold and I hate the treadmill, so I take the winters off. I guess that works toward my ultimate goal of still running when I'm seventy, but it means a slow start in the spring, rebuilding mileage and speed. Typically my November 5K times are two or three minutes faster than my March times.

One year, I had hopes of running a half marathon late in the season. That's thirteen miles. Three times I made it to ten miles. Now, ten miles is nothing to sneeze at, but when I couldn't make my goal times for ten miles, I didn't sign up for the half.

The next year, I signed up for a ten-mile race. In the spring. Even though the weather had been terribly uncooperative. Even though I was starting to transition from "I can do this," to "What was I thinking?" Even though it was the very thing I failed at the previous summer.

Runners are fond of saying, **Trust the training.** In other words, you trust that the little things you've been doing everyday have adequately prepared you for race day. My husband even told me after a six-mile run, "If you can do six, you can do ten."

I wasn't so sure. I knew how I felt at the end of six. He assured me that the training would kick in, and that I was better prepared than I realized.

As believers, God will often put things on our hearts— goals, hopes, dreams, ministries—things we don't feel prepared for, maybe that we feel totally inadequate for. Because of that, more often than not, we close the door. The opportunity passes and we ignore the tug inside until it fades away.

But those situations are the very ones that showcase God's power and not our own abilities. Not only that, we see what God has been building in us all along.

It's up to us to trust the training, and ultimately the Trainer when He says we can handle ten, even if we think six is really pushing it.

Is there something you've felt God nudging you toward? Is it time to trust the training and the Trainer?

Six Lessons from the River Run

> *Finally, there is laid up for me the crown of righteousness, which the Lord, the righteous Judge, will give to me on that Day, and not to me only but also to all who have loved His appearing. 2 Timothy 4:8*

I'm not a very good runner. I told you that up front. And I'm even worse at races than I am at running around in the mornings. Even so, my husband and I ran the Evansville River Run. It's a ten-mile race starting in Henderson, Kentucky, crossing the Ohio River Bridge and finishing in Evansville, Indiana. Talk about a learning experience ... And all of the lessons apply to the race I'm running in my Christian life.

1. You think you're prepared ...

Training runs are a whole different ballgame from a race. The course was hillier than I was used to. I overdressed. (That was a calculated risk. I hate, hate being cold.) Running by the highway is mentally fatiguing.

We often think that after a weekly church service, we're prepared for whatever gets thrown at us, but we're often surprised by circumstances. Situations often prove more challenging than we imagined and we discover that theory and life are two different things. We need to make sure we are relying on God in humility and not trusting ourselves.

2. I started strong and finished strong. The middle . . . not so much.

Through the first six miles I was on pace to do better than any of my training runs. Then reality struck. And by reality, I mean pain. Everything hurt except for my hair and my eyebrows. And my hair was close. I chose to ease off on my pace and finish well rather than risk a real injury. My last 400m was my fastest all day.

We usually start out strong, really gung-ho for Jesus, but somewhere in the middle of things we run into some painful times. It is extremely important to back off and give yourself time to rest and heal so you can stay in the race and finish strong.

3. Having folks cheer you on is awesome.

I have no idea who most of them were but it was a little easier to run with some encouragement, especially from the little guy who high-fived me toward the end and my son and a really good friend near the finish.

We really underestimate the value of encouragement in the body of Christ. It can help prevent burning out, dropping out and falling out. Let's resolve not to be so stingy with it.

4. Having someone come along beside to run with you is even awesome-r.

My husband finished forty minutes before I did, but he came back and met me at mile nine and finished with me. I told him everything hurt. He reminded me that my pace wasn't bad, that in twelve more minutes we'd be done, that the finish wasn't nearly as far away as it looked, that he was proud of me . . . all kinds of good stuff.

We not only have fellow believers to come alongside us, but God Himself is right there in the person of the Holy Spirit offering guidance and encouragement.

5. The effects last way beyond the race.

The race was Saturday. It was Tuesday before I could walk down steps without turning sideways.

Make no mistake, the things we do in this life will have an impact on eternity.

6. Finishing is what counts.

Oh, sure the guy who won finished in less than half the time that I did, but you know what? I got the very same medal he got. All the finishers did.

There is coming a day when we will each cross a finish line and receive a reward. I haven't seen it, but I'm pretty sure it's a lot better than a medal.

Have you done something that stretched you? What lessons did you learn?

Faith Not Comfort

I have been crucified with Christ; it is no longer I who live, but Christ lives in me; and the life which I now live in the flesh I live by faith in the Son of God, who loved me and gave Himself for me. Galatians 2:20

There was one winter when I didn't run very much at all. It was cold. Ridiculously, record-shatteringly cold. The kind of cold that makes you forget things like air conditioning . . .and short sleeves . . . and grass. I may be exaggerating a little, but not much. But I digress.

This is how running happens for me. I run around five a.m. Nobody is out, or if they are, they're either too sleepy to notice me, or they're busy with their own running. Perfect. I hate being cold so if it dips below twenty-five or thirty degrees, I don't go out. I don't like being wet either, so rain is a deal breaker. Oh, and treadmills make me dizzy. I don't typically run on Saturdays, because that's my husband's day to run and I don't want to go off and leave my kids asleep. I can't use an mp3 player because I have to be able to hear killer dogs sneaking up behind me. And owls. Besides all that, I have to make sure I choose streets that are well-lit because except for about six weeks or so in the summer, it's dark when I run.

It's a wonder I ever get any miles logged, isn't it? I will never be a great runner because I just do it for fun (and because exercise is good for me). If it's not fun or satisfying, I'm not going to put the effort into it. Period.

Most of the time, I approach following Christ the very same way. I want it to be on my schedule, on my terms and at my convenience. I want it to be comfortable and satisfying without being painful and strenuous. I want to do enough to look and sound legit, especially when other followers are around.

That's not what Christ called me to. And that's not the call I answered.

Paul explains in Galatians 2:20, *I have been crucified with Christ. It is no longer I who live, but Christ who lives in me. And the life I now live in the flesh I live by faith in the Son of God, who loved me and gave himself for me.*

Following Christ means I need to live by faith, not by comfort. It means I need to actively choose faith over comfort. And it means there is a great gap between where I should be and where I am.

But He loved me and He gave Himself for me, so I can't quit. Even for a month or two. Even if it's cold out.

(In my defense, I did a 30-Day Ab Challenge during those frigid days, which meant more muscles hurt than I realized I possessed, and I discovered I am the worst sit-upper ever. I was glad to run again.)

How can we keep from getting comfortable in our faith? Have you ever given God conditions or parameters for your obedience? Why do you think we want those caveats?

Quiet Miles

My soul, wait silently for God alone, for my expectation is from Him. Psalm 62:5

Sometime running seasons are quiet. Only one race. No speed records. No personal bests. Just miles.

The only folks who know I'm out there are my husband and a few other runners. And the dogs that bark. Lots of dogs.

Some seasons in our Christian lives are that way. We do our quiet work in the background. We read and study. We pray.

Nothing flashy or remarkable. No new ministries. Just consistency.

Those quiet seasons can be very good things. Here are some things I've noticed happening during this quiet season.

I've built endurance. In February, four miles is long. In the summer, it's an easy day. It's during the quiet seasons that we build patience and endurance in our faith as we wait and watch for God's next assignment.

What seemed difficult before may be a little less challenging as we developed greater intimacy and dependence on Jesus.

I've lost weight. When I put in the miles, it's a natural result. In the same way, if we put in the time and effort into growing our faith, the natural result will be shedding unhealthy ideas and attitudes that hold us back or hinder us completely.

I've developed a habit. I miss it when I don't run. My day feels "off" and I feel guilty. It's in the quiet times that we cultivate a habit of talking to God, hearing from Him, soaking in His presence. Skipping out on that time can throw off or whole day.

I also know what I still need to work on. I get really tired after about five miles, so I'll be experimenting with snacks either the night before or before I leave the house. My pace is not where I'd like it to be, so I'll be focusing on that too. Likewise, it's in quiet times that Jesus can offer help with our weaknesses or encourage us with new visions and goals.

What things have you learned in the quiet seasons? Are they necessary for growth? Should they be intentional?

Community

Now you are the body of Christ, and members individually. 1 Corinthians 12:27

Even though I run by myself early in the morning, I'm not alone as a runner. I have friends who run and even family members who run. It's good to have those connections because, believe me, you don't get too many miles logged before a host of questions pop up.

Should I rest or run through the pain? (That is, is this a real injury or am I just a baby?) What's the best way to work up to a longer distance? How do I tell when I need new shoes? Is Gu really worth it?

No matter what questions I come up with, some runner I know has the answer. They've been through it and they are more than willing to share what they've learned.

Oh, **I could figure things out on my own**, but in the end, I'd make more mistakes. I'd be injured more often, and for longer periods. By learning everything the hard way, I'd spend less time actually running.

For some reason, **that's the way we operate as believers. On our own. Muddling through. Figuring things out the best way we can**. Maybe we're afraid people will find out we don't have it all together. Maybe we're afraid we'll look weak. Or sinful.

So we keep quiet. We don't ask. We pretend like we know everything. We never have problems. And we miss out on one of the greatest blessings God gave us.

Community.

In the Greek, the word is *ekklesia*, and until the time of Christ, it meant any assembly people were called to, like a town hall gathering. Usually, we translate the word "church" and keep reading. The first-century followers of Christ redefined the very word by the way they connected and treated each other.

We need each other, far more than we realize. We need to share our stories and our struggles. We need to testify about how God is working in our lives. We need to be a blessing and an encouragement. We need safety and transparency and vulnerability.

Within a community, we build the relationships and the love that Christ meant for us to have for one another.

It is from a community that we launch out on the Great Commission.

A group of unique individuals transforming into a community of brothers and sisters is the sure witness of God's power at work in us.

Who is part of your community? What do you contribute and what benefits do you receive? Why do you think God wants us in a community rather than operating on our own?

Simple Pleasures

Cause me to hear Your lovingkindness in the morning, For in You do I trust; Cause me to know the way in which I should walk, For I lift up my soul to You. Psalm 143:8

When I run, I use an app on my phone that tracks my distance, time and pace. In preparation for an upcoming race, I started using the coaching feature. I set it for the pace I want to run and every minute it lets me know how I'm doing. "9:52. You're ahead of your pace. Slow down. Great job!" Or, "12:15. You're behind your goal pace. Speed up. Awesome workout!"

Now the programmers could have left the 'awesome workout' part off when I'm behind pace. But I think they left it for a purpose. I tend to get focused on results, on my ability or failure to meet one goal or another. The 'awesome workout' reminder points me to something broader. Being out alone in the morning quiet is a good thing.

Not only that, simply being able to run is a gift and a blessing. I shouldn't lose those simple pleasures because the number on a pace meter wasn't what I thought it should be.

I get that same kind of narrow view in my Christian walk as well. I set standards for how I think I should be progressing. (Notice, I set them, not God.) Then I have to start monitoring. Am I on pace with the right number of quiet times? Did I read enough chapters? Did I meet my goal for prayer? Or study? Or growth? Am I closer to God than I was last week? Am I on pace or behind?

Now I believe **a periodic spiritual inventory can be a good thing, but not an end in itself.** For me, I find that in the quest to meet some goal or achieve a metric, I completely miss the joy, the gift, the blessing that comes with a relationship with Christ. It's a relationship guided by His timing and not my schedule, founded on His grace and not my performance.

Which "metrics" do tend to focus on? What helps you refocus on Jesus and your relationship with Him?

Abide

I am the vine, you are the branches. He who abides in Me, and I in him, bears much fruit; for without Me you can do nothing. John 15:5

One bright June Saturday, my husband, my son and I ran an obstacle course race. Now what I absolutely don't want you to do is read that and think I'm some kind of super athlete. Because I'm not. I was just following through on something that sounded like a great idea back in January when we were eating Pizza Hut and watching football. Anybody can compete, they said. If you can walk five miles you can finish this race. This one was three weeks after the 10 mile River Run. I figured I was good to go.

Well, yes it's five miles. Through the woods. Up and down hills. Through creeks and mud. Then every so often they throw in some obstacle, like the Confidence Wall or the Delta Cargo Tower or the Wreck Bag Carry, or more mud, just to keep it interesting.

But what makes this race different is that you are allowed, even encouraged, to help each other. And quite frankly, if my husband had not stuck with me, I wouldn't have finished the course. He walked ahead of me, constantly giving me feedback. "Stay to the left. The mud's not as deep. It's slick there. Grab here to pull yourself up." He gave me a boost when I was too short to reach the first foothold on the 8-foot wall, then he ran around to the other side, so I could grab his shoulder and not have to drop so far. He sacrificed his time and final ranking to make sure I reached the finish line.

Wow, what an object lesson.

In John 15 as Jesus is giving His last teaching before the cross He tells them plainly, "Without Me, you can do nothing." On the other hand, if they abide in Him, and by extension, if we abide in Him, we bear fruit. Lots of it.

Abide is one of those words we pretend like we know what it means and we read over it. So I looked it up. It has a range of meanings.

1. **To wait for** – I waited for Jon to go ahead of me in the race. I wait to follow Jesus's leading.

2. **To withstand, to bear patiently** – I had to get through some killer obstacles. Jesus is going to throw some challenges my way as well.

3. **To accept without objection** – Signing up for the race meant following the course laid out. If Jesus is Lord like I say He is, I follow where He leads.

4. **To remain stable in a state** – I didn't follow Jon for a bit, then follow somebody else. By the same token, I need to stick with Jesus the whole way.

The Message translates *abide* as "joined with" and then elaborates, "the relation intimate and organic." It was completely natural for me to trust Jon and look to him for help, because of our relationship. How much more naturally should I trust and follow Jesus?

See, I don't run because I'm good at it. Far from it. Honestly, it was Wednesday before I could walk up and down steps without a lot of pain. Running always teaches me something, though. Always. In this case, it's a lesson that will stick with me even longer than the mud. (It's never washing out... Never.)

(And in case you were wondering, my son ran his own race, finished #28 in the killer 15-19 age group.)

Is abiding in Christ difficult? Is one area, like remaining or accepting more difficult? How could someone come alongside and help you? How might you help someone else?

Revival

Revive me according to Your lovingkindness, so that I may keep the testimony of Your mouth. Psalm 119:88

Can I be really honest? My most recent running season was not my best. I ran a couple of good races in the spring, but through the summer and fall, I was something less than enthusiastic. I found a lot of excuses. I didn't put out my best effort. Really, I ended up with nothing but sweaty clothes to show for my trek outside.

Then I had some routine bloodwork done. Elevated HA1C. Borderline diabetes. It wasn't a complete surprise. I know my genetic makeup, and I had gestational diabetes when I carried my son. My risk is above average. Running immediately became more significant, and more of a priority. I had a renewed sense of purpose and commitment to it. When it came to running, I experienced a revival.

I find I need revival often on my walk with Jesus, and more often than the traditional spring and fall series of meetings. Just like a blood test can alert me to some physiological issues, there are a couple of markers that alert me to deeper spiritual ones.

Lack of compassion – When I find I'm more inwardly focused and tending to ignore the hurting people around me, that's a warning sign.

Lack of engagement – When I find I'm not mentally present in worship or in my study time or during prayers, that's a wake-up call.

The solution is two-fold.

Just like my HA1C results require a change in diet, revival does, too. **I need to change what I'm consuming** whether it's media or the attitudes or ideas of others. Instead, I need to take in generous servings of truth, seeing people the way God sees them.

Then **I need to be more intentional about my walk with Jesus**. I need to remind myself of His majesty and holiness and greatness, and the wonder of His amazing love for me. The more I honor God in worship the easier it is to follow Him in obedience.

In a few months I'll have my blood checked again, then I can find out how I've done and if further changes are necessary. I don't have to wait that long to see how I'm progressing on my walk. The Holy Spirit will nudge and encourage me at each step. I just have to make sure I'm listening and making the changes He asks of me.

What about you? Do you need a revival? How do you know?
What steps do you take to begin a personal revival?

COVENANT OF TRUST SERIES

Faith and real life meet head on in the Covenant of Trust series and *CONTINGENCY* is where it all begins. If you want characters you instantly connect with, authentic struggles that are raw, honest, and platitude-free, wrapped in a story that pulls you in and won't let go, you want *CONTINGENCY*. Pick it up. You won't put it down.

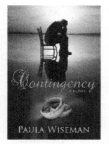

A Betrayal Exposed. A Shattered Marriage. A Step of Faith.

Bobbi Molinsky had it all--a successful husband, two great boys and a job she loved-- then she opens a stray email from the newest attorney at Chuck's firm, and is blindsided by the discovery of his extramarital affair. An angry confrontation leaves her with the broken remains of their eighteen-year marriage. Caught between a crisis of faith and her deepest fears, trust is a risk she can't afford to take.

Book 2
INDEMNITY
Tracy Ravenna returns and that covenant is threatened from the outside.

Book 3
PRECEDENT
That covenant is tested to its limits as Chuck wonders if he can ever make things right.

Book 4
SANCTION
The covenant brings the past and present together and sets the course for the future.

FOUNDATIONS SERIES

In the Foundations series, the characters discover exactly what they've built their lives on. Sometimes those foundations prove firm and true. At other times, they crumble under the weight of life's trials and burdens. Each story, each situation brings the reader face-to-face with the questions, "What have I built my life on? Will I stand or crumble?"

In RAZED, we meet Doug Bolling.

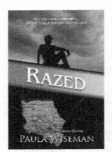

A God who lets a 40-year-old woman die from cancer can't be good. That's Doug's theology. He can't seem to connect with his son, Mark, who found Jesus because of his mother. The more Mark grows in his faith, the wider the rift becomes. A series of events in Mark's life, from a call to preach, to a pastorate, to seminary, to the mission field are utterly incomprehensible to Doug, and he interprets them as extremism bordering on insanity. God may have ripped away his wife and now his son, but Doug draws the line at his grandchildren. In a desperate attempt to snatch them back from a life of who knows what, he files a lawsuit, seeking custody of the children.

In *REFINED*, Mark has been obedient to God's call every step of the way, but now God issues the most difficult challenge of all—surrendering his children. When Doug files a custody suit, Mark and his family are forced to leave the mission field in Kenya and come home for the legal battle of a lifetime.

RESOLUTE is a story of holding on to faith even when it leads in a direction you never anticipated, and requires more than you want to give. Doug is diagnosed with Alzheimer's disease and his and Mark's relationship must undergo a final adjustment. Mark gives up the mission in Africa for his father.

56 Tips: To Help You Get the Most Out of Every Book in the Bible

No matter if you are a beginner or long-time student of Scripture, 56 TIPS TO HELP YOU GET THE MOST OUT OF EVERY BOOK IN THE BIBLE will provide a framework for your personal study time.

In a compact format, 56 TIPS gives

- background notes,
- keywords,
- things to look for,
- questions to consider

for each book demonstrating the accessibility of God's word.

ABOUT THE AUTHOR

Author, blogger, and speaker Paula Wiseman has over twenty years'
experience as a Bible teacher, and eight years' experience as a runner.
She is the author of several award-winning Christian fiction
bestsellers, including the Covenant of Trust series, featuring
Contingency. Find out more at www.paulawiseman.com.

Made in the USA
Monee, IL
23 February 2023

28519891R00059